To the friends you'll meet
& to those that will
take your breath away.

Carpe Diem!

Rico

Dedicated to man's best friend.
my best friend,
Sir Princeton!

Let's take a trip to a special place
To greet a friend with a warm embrace.
A wonderful place filled with love,
Full of God's grace from up above.

A place of wonder and magic carpet rides
A special place with love on all sides.
Get in your race cars so you won't be late
To find out what makes a best friend great.

Let's close our eyes and there we'll see
two best friends: Princeton and me!

He was pure breed Maltese
Wore a royal robe with a golden fleece.
He was no more than 16 inches long,
But I swear he stood 10 feet tall.

He grew on me — like a flame of fire
Always together, true love never tires.

He got really sick as a pup
But we swore to never give up.
We battled through everything that hurt
With prayers, persistence, and pure effort.

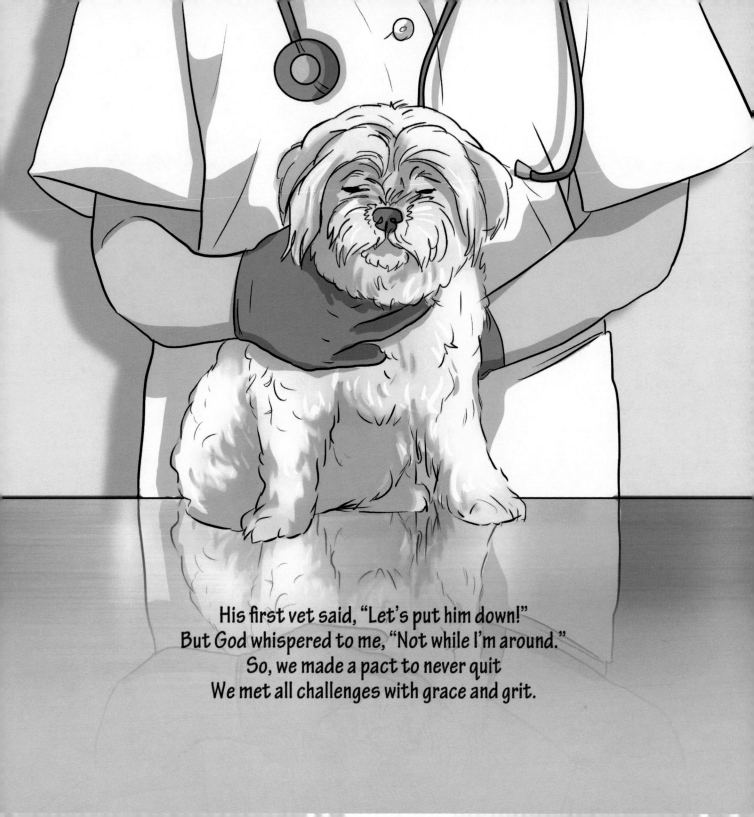

His first vet said, "Let's put him down!"
But God whispered to me, "Not while I'm around."
So, we made a pact to never quit
We met all challenges with grace and grit.

My shadow, my friend, my 6 o'clock.
Best friends forever around the clock.
No days off, no days wasted,
No sweeter joy I've ever tasted.

I'd be remiss if I did not mention
All the things he could do with the power of Princeton!
X-ray vision and super strength
Shoot a bow and arrow endless lengths!

He leapt great walls and flew on wings.
Could run super-fast, could do all things.
He climbed tall buildings
in a single bound.
Threw 100 mph from
the pitching mound.
He moved mountains
and swam lakes.
Could do it all,
whatever it takes.

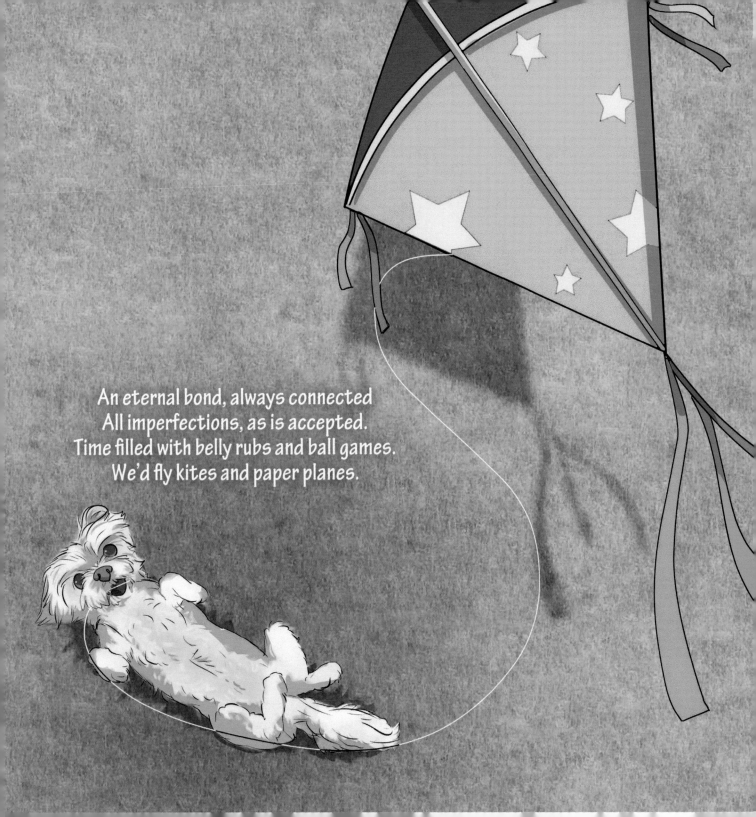

An eternal bond, always connected
All imperfections, as is accepted.
Time filled with belly rubs and ball games.
We'd fly kites and paper planes.

One for all, and Princeton for me
My dear sweet friend, he was family.
All who knew and touched him, loved him
Magnetic love, no friend above him.

I travelled far for business but flew back late and drove by night
all to be right by his side.
Thunder buddies and super friends,
Caped crusaders saving the end!
Tag Team Champions, best duo ever
Princeton and me, through all endeavors.

He got lost twice but always made it back home.
He knew his place was next to me all along.
Lost Doggie signs promised no questions asked.
A $300 reward ensured he'd
come home fast.

LOST DOG

$300 REWARD!
"PRINCETON"

He seized many times
but seized the day most,
day trips together,
stops by the coast.

He fell down 7 times, but got up 8
A true warrior at Heaven's gate.
8 lbs., 8 ounces of pure might
No ailment could ever slow his fight.

He overcame so many things —
from rashes to bumps, and all things in between.
But no complaints, no whimpers or whines,
No tougher friend,
best friend of mine.

We tried to solve the puzzle of his health
But some ailments are blessings, best handled in stealth.
Some problems, some pains, are bigger than us.
Best left to prayer, understanding, and unconditional love.

My best friend never drove me
home or picked up the tab.
Never followed me on social media
or grabbed a cab,
But he made me feel
like a king every day
Like I could take on the world,
hold time at bay
Sun of his solar system,
center of his world
I see him running in my mind,
never ending twirl!

Halloweens and Christmas Days
All days Thanksgiving,
all days were birthdays!
I'd come home to the
greatest reception.
A bark, a chase, a special
dance to get my
attention.

He'd always wait for me to eat
Alfredo with chicken, his favorite treat.
He also loved chow mein and cheesecake
A late-night taco, chicken with steak.

He got really sick
as an elder
But we swore to
never surrender.
Power of love,
power of perseverance
Power of friendship,
power of Princeton!

A dream come true.
Gift from above.
He was pure joy and
was pure love.
So that's the essence of
my best friend
The heart of a lion,
my sweet Princeton.

A wise man said, "The measure of love is to love without measure"
And that was him, my little reflection, my greatest treasure.

Princeton + Me

What did I learn from him?
So many things . . .
Love always, be kind,
and do great things.
Never give up; never surrender
Life tests the strong.
Endure. Conquer forever!
Be true, authentic,
and strong.
Seize the day, Carpe diem!
Forever long.
Release your gifts
into the world
Use passion and purpose
as your chief tools.
And persist, no matter what!

Overcome obstacles
no matter your lot.
No dog's too big or too small
True friendship endures,
love conquers all!
Be a Prince or Princess,
Live with love and joy.
What a great teacher,
good boy, good boy!

Oh, where, oh where might his place be?!
It will always be inside of me.
Through thick and thin, until the end,
no better friend, has ever been.
Cherished memories and times spent,
with my best friend, Sir Princeton.

A sum that's greater than our parts
I'll see you soon, no time apart,
All dogs go to heaven, I'll look to the skies
I'll see you soon, never goodbye.

A friend of a lifetime, never to be forgotten
The best friend now, of the Begotten.

I'll see you soon over the rainbow bridge.
In God's green pastures, playing on the pitch.
I'll close my eyes, and see your face
and I'll always remember my Princeton's Place.